Blackcurrant Jam

Written by Louise Spilsbury
Photographed by Will Amlot

Collins

Let's cook blackcurrant jam.

You can pick blackcurrants in the summer.

First, get a little blackcurrant tree from a garden shop.

Put it out in the garden, in the sun.

Sunlight will help it get bigger!

The little tree needs food, too.
Put compost all around
its roots.

compost

The tree will suck up rain with its roots. The roots will travel out and down into the soil.

roots

Soon little buds form.

The days get longer and heat up. Each leaf and bud gets bigger. Little flowers appear. The blackcurrant tree gets stronger.

Bees come to suck nectar from the flowers.

Soon, blackcurrants will start to form!

When the blackcurrants start to turn from green to black, put a net on them. This will keep the birds away.

Pick the blackcurrants one by one when they are deep black and still firm.

Now you can cook some jam!

You need to pull off all the stems.

Then tip the blackcurrants into a big pan.
Simmer until the blackcurrant skins
are tender.

Stir the pan so the blackcurrants do not stick to the bottom.

Now add in some sweetness and some lemon.

lemon

Boil the blackcurrant mix.
An adult must help you with this,
as the jam will get hot!

Let the jam cool.
Then tip it into jars.

Add a sticker to each jam jar.
This sticker has blackcurrants on it.

Now you can eat the jam. Put some on toast, or on a bun.

Enjoy it!

From blackcurrants to jam

Review: After reading

Use your assessment from hearing the children read to choose any GPCs, words or tricky words that need additional practice.

Read 1: Decoding

- Turn to page 10. Ask the children to find the word **turn**, and show you the letters that make the /ur/ sound. (*ur*)
- Can the children find another word on page 10 that has the /ur/ sound? (*birds*)
- Talk about the way the /ur/ sound is spelled in this word. (*ir*)
- Now look for more words in the book that have the /ur/ sound spelled "ir". (*first, stir, firm*)

Read 2: Prosody

- Choose two double page spreads and model reading with expression to the children.
- Ask the children to have a go at reading the same pages with expression.

Read 3: Comprehension

- For every question ask the children how they know the answer. Ask:
  o What do the blackcurrant plants need in order to grow? (*light/sun, food/compost, water/rain*)
  o What are the different stages in making jam? (*pour the blackcurrants into the pan, simmer, stir, add sweetness/sugar and lemon, boil, let it cool, pour into jars*)
  o Would you like to make jam? Why or why not?
  o If yes, what type of jam would you make?